# Here's what people are saying about PAPOLíTICO

"If someone claims they married Puerto Rico, it means they must have married the poet, Papoleto, who is the essence of the island, its people, struggles, dignity, music and dance. Not in a very long time has a son of Borinquen unearth its history and its foilables, from romance to politics of this enchanted harried nation as Papoleto has done in this collection, PAPOLíTICO!"

—Ntozake Shange, poet, writer, and author of the classic choreopoem,
*for colored girls who have considered suicide / when the rainbows is enuf* (1977)

"Papo's latest poetry collection, PAPOLíTICO, does not allow even the most progressive or the most radical of us to get away with the hypocrisy of simply living and getting by. Papo's verses stalk you in midday, throw you up against the wall of indifference in the alley of numbing conformity, and pummels you into feeling the pain of folks, conditions you've trained yourself to ignore. His metaphors demand you swallow the fetid water of racism, the rancid meat of capitalism, the insidious candy of nihilism, and forces us to think of what we've become as a nation. PAPOLíTICO also reminds us that someone is still watching for us, feeling for us, living for us, all with the hope that we rise and resist and love again."

—Felipe Luciano, poet, community activist, journalist, and lecturer

"I truly appreciate where Papoleto is coming from politically, and his latest book, PAPOLíTICO, has been aptly named. I love his sense of humor and of course, his sarcasm – he is good and crazy! What's important here is that Papoleto deals with the pain, the love, and the uncertainties of life as only a true poet could. From the first poem to the last, it's clear that he lives and breathes poetry naturally. It was a real pleasure reading PAPOLíTICO, and traveling into the mind and soul of a tender human being."

—Abiodun Oyewole, The Last Poets.
author of *Branches of the Tree of Life* (2014) and *The Beauty of Being* (2018)

# PAPOLÍTICO

P.O. Box 4378
Grand Central Station
New York, New York 10163-4378
editor@2leafpress.org
www.2leafpress.org

2LEAF PRESS
is an imprint of the
Intercultural Alliance of Artists & Scholars, Inc. (IAAS),
a NY-based nonprofit 501(c)(3) organization that promotes
multicultural literature and literacy.
www.theiaas.org

*Book design and layout:* Gabrielle David

*Poetry editor:* Sean Dillon

Library of Congress Control Number: 2017963103

ISBN-13: 978-1-940939-73-5 (Paperback)
ISBN-13: 978-1-940939-88-9 (eBook)

10  9  8  7  6  5  4  3  2  1

Published in the United States of America

First Edition | First Printing

2LEAF PRESS trade distribution is handled by University of Chicago Press / Chicago Distribution Center (www.press.uchicago.edu) 773.702.7010. Titles are also available for corporate, premium, and special sales. Please direct inquiries to the UCP Sales Department, 773.702.7248.

*This collection is dedicated to*
*the belief that The Nature of Poetry*
*is the Universal Empathetic Expression*
*of the Spirits' suffering a Human Experience.*

*At the risk of seeming ridiculous, let me say that the true revolutionary is guided by a great feeling of love. It is impossible to think of a genuine revolutionary lacking this quality.*

—Ernesto Che Guevara
"Socialism and man" in Cuba, March 12, 1965,
under the title, "From Algiers, for Marcha, The Cuban Revolution Today"

*It is only a matter of time until the question of the prisoner's debt to society versus society's debt to the prisoner is injected forcefully into national and state politics, into the civil and human right struggle, and into the consciousness of the body politic.*

—Eldridge Cleaver, *Soul on Ice* (1968)

*Hence I have no mercy or compassion in me for a society that will crush people, and then penalize them for not being able to stand up under the weight.*

—Malcolm X, *The Autobiography of Malcolm X* (1965)

*¡La Patria Es Valor y Sacrificio!*
*(The Motherland is Valor and Sacrifice!)*

—Don Pedro Albizu Campos
The Nationalist Party's 1932 national elections' slogan

*¡Yo no vine a matar a nadie, yo vine a morir por Puerto Rico!*
*(I did not come to kill anyone, I came to die for Puerto Rico!)*

—Lolita Lebron
when arrested in Washington, D.C. on March 1, 1954

# THE POEMS

❖ ❖ ❖

PREFACE ❖ vii

INTRODUCTION ❖ 1

INDENTURED . . . 9

A COP HAIKU . . . 10

HUMAN WISDOM . . . 11

MEDIOCRYSIS . . . 15

STORY FROM A MOUNTAIN . . . 21

FOR THE ANGEL DIAZES . . . 25

SUBWAY SLEEPER CAR SLEEPER . . . 29

AGAINST THE THREAT OF AIDS . . . 33

TOURISM UP+DOW/JONES, 6PTS. . . . 39

SUICIDALSOCIETALITY . . . 41

A CONVERSATION WITH A BLIND MAN . . . 47

UNITY SPEAK . . . . . . 61

BASEBALL FEVER . . . 62

THE MILLION YOUTH MARCH #1 . . . 63

BEAT WHITE DUDE . . . 65

DRAMA ON T.V. . . . 69

A SAN DIEGO SOUTHERN/AFRICAN NIGHT . . . 73

ELOQUENT HYPOCRISY . . . 91

JADED ON JADE . . . 99

KILLKILLKILL . . . 103

THE FLOOD CAME TO PUERTO RICO . . . 109

TO PAY A NATIONAL DEBT— TO PUERTO RICO
OSCAR LÓPEZ-RIVERA MUST BE SET FREE IMMEDIATELY! . . . 111

A CONVERSATION WITH MY SON . . . 117

FAIR FOR FARE . . . 119

OVERFLOW . . . 121

ACKNOWLEDGEMENTS ❖ 123

ABOUT THE POET ❖ 127

CONTRIBUTORS ❖ 131

OTHER BOOKS BY 2LEAF PRESS ❖ 133

It was my long-time friend and collaborator, Bernardo Palombo, Argentinean composer of "Nova Trova" (protest lyrics in song), founder and Executive Director of El Taller Latino Americano, who expressed to me that much of my poetry seemed political in nature, and that I should consider titling a performance or other work, "PAPOLÍTICO." Thanks, brother Bernardo.

# PREFACE

❖ ❖ ❖

**IT SEEMS TO ME** that in my early development as a poet, it took quite a while to start writing "politically." However, when I review my big brown leather book where my poems are logged in the chronological order as they were created, the reader almost immediately becomes aware of social consciousness, replete in even my adolescent observations.

I remember a time during the presidential campaign of November 1960, when I was a nine-year-old Puerto Rican kid living in El Barrio, East Harlem, attending public school. The day after the election, our teacher posed the question, "Last night, John Fitzgerald Kennedy was elected to be the president of what?" I eagerly raised my hand, confident that I was certain of the correct answer. When the teacher picked me, I snapped back, "President of the world!" My teacher laughed out loud, and said that I was wrong. She picked another student, who answered, "The President of the United States of America." I was floored. I was so sure that Kennedy had been elected president of the world, and was disappointed that he wasn't.

So even back then, my political perspective, though somewhat obscure, was a visceral rather than intellectual, experience for me. It's hypocrisy, the parent of all evil that irritates me the most because it is an ironic interplay of self-righteousness. Thus, the ironic moment, which is found in most of my poetry, has become the inspirational spark from which my imagination and sense of social conviction merge.

I believe that this is where I'm always coming from when I approach a subject poetically. My poems are "still-life" vignettes of a moment in time imbued within its hypocrisy.

Welcome to the land of PAPOLÍTICO.❖

*Papo*

# INTRODUCTION

❖  ❖  ❖

**IN THE MID-1980S**, some years into our sojourn in San Diego, we met a young Puerto Rican poet named Jesús Papoleto Meléndez. At the time he was living in Tijuana in an artist's co-op behind a café called El Nopal. His street-loving verses were tapped out on an old Royal typewriter, which he made into chapbooks and sold on the very streets that inspired them. The poems, like Papoleto, bounced and tumbled down the margins that were at odds with literary order and local authority.

Papoleto's poetry weaves through city streets like a feral cat — passing walls with unexpected tags and sun glinting alleys of truth. In his sixth volume of poetry, PAPOLíTICO, Papoleto does just that. It is an exciting compilation of new and previously published poems designed to nudge people out of complacency. Papoleto speaks truth to power. Defying the political and media rhetoric that is designed to obscure and manipulate us. PAPOLíTICO marks this moment of political rupture by summoning the collective strength found in the language of resistance and memory, subversion and declamation, struggle and hope, with poetry. Throughout this volume, Papoleto reminds us why poetry remains a necessary medium in moments of political crisis and social consciousness.

Poets are always, at some level, writing about current events, by way of personal, emotional, intellectual, or cultural forces that have led to those events. What's interesting about PAPOLíTICO is that some of the works written twenty or thirty years ago continue to speak to the very issues we see today, rendering the poems timeless and incredibly prescient, but timeless.  For example, in "A Conversation with a Blind Man" (p. 47), first published in 1993, Papoleto exclaims:

> He's locked
> his mind's door
> /Against the face
> of a society
> of hoards

(p.54)

Another example is "The Flood Came to Puerto Rico" (p. 109). Papoleto speaks of the devastating flood in 1971 in Puerto Rico. He sees this weather event with a wide angle lens, tying the flood to the Rockefeller family's land holdings on the island. Their wealth and plans for tourist development necessitate the strict law and order policies that continue to repress Puerto Ricans today. In that very year of the poem's creation, the family heir, New York's Governor Nelson Rockefeller reacted to the Attica prison uprising with vicious brutality against prisoners and guards alike, as corrections officers and the National Guard retook the prison. It is as ironic as it is sad that the original context of a poem written over forty years ago remains intact, and the Rockefeller reference was simply changed to "Donald Trump":

"the flood came to Puerto Rico/
& with it came the red cross
                    /after the flood
to search for Donald Trump's golf courses
                    & summer homes."
(p. 110)

Papoleto is not a poet in a garret, but a vibrant community activist. Over the years, his poetry has traversed from New York, to San Diego and Mexico, and to New York again, with intermittent visits to Puerto Rico. He has given poetry a key role in barrio life on both coasts. As one of the founders of the Nuyorican Movement, Papoleto has always supported the idea that the arts is a form of activism that exists in a system that continuously attempts to drown people out.

When Papoleto lived in the San Diego/Tijuana region, he was a Nuyorican ambassador to the Chicano and Mexican communities. We remember when Papoleto read his poetry at the "Che Café" and at the legendary events at the La Jolla Museum/UCSD curated by Quincy Troupe and Margaret Porter. He organized a musical trio, "Exiled Genius," with Eugene Mingus and M'Chaka Uba performing at the Centro Cultural de la Raza in Balboa Park and El Nopal in Tijuana. From the moment we met, we became close friends and over the years, and have supported Papoleto's work.

When he returned to New York and to El Barrio (East Harlem) in the early 1990s, the Nuyorican and Black Arts movements had morphed into a multicultural movement. While Papoleto continued to write and perform poetry with a wider worldview, his personal observations were often framed around his life in New York. As he takes a ride on the subway, rumbling underground and observing a sleeping subway rider, Papoleto captures the moment in "Subway Sleeper Car Sleeper" (p. 29):

"Sometimes, Someone's life
                    just
    *falls* right down;
            (and so,
                one needs to take a nap)
                            in Life…"

(p.29)

Another subway poem, "Fair for Fare" (p. 119), Papoleto intertwines city living and city survival in echoed reverberation:

"The roaring railing
                wheels
        against the steel
                of Reality
                    & Life—
    Against a will
            Against the wind,
        Against the word
                Against the world."

(p.120)

Papoleto's poems hold the distinction of incorporating his immediate environment into his work, becoming "one" with his surroundings. That's why you can tell the difference between a San Diego and New York poem: "place" plays an important role in his work.

Papoleto has always said that to be a poet is a condition, not a profession, and that there is a difference between a poet, and someone who writes good poems. A poet is an active participant in life, incorporating daily experiences into meaningful expression. Since we have known Papoleto for almost forty years, and have had the pleasure of witnessing this poet-activist in action, we understand the importance of connecting the dots of his early work to the ongoing evolution of his unique literary activism so clearly evident in the poems contained in this volume.

Besides his involvement in the Nuyorican and Black Arts movements, Papoleto has been engaged in various forms of activism for over forty years. These include marches, counter marches, and on the ground actions, as well as organizing and teaching. As a frequent participant in the artists-in-schools programs in both San Diego and New York, Papoleto has introduced hundreds of young people to poetry. He also published quite a few student anthologies to memorialize their participation. These anthologies were never casual affairs for Papoleto, but the product of many all-nighters on his computer, carefully arranging their poems into small books to be treasured by these young authors.

He supported Puerto Rican political prisoners such as Dylcia Pagán and Oscar Lopez Rivera, who have spent decades in the Federal Penitentiary for their support for Puerto Rican independence. He was vocal in the struggle to remove the U.S. military from the island of Vieques, traveling to Puerto Rico with his comrade, Pedro Pietri, to stand up to U.S. intervention.

Papoleto has consistently lent his voice and support to numerous community issues, working closely with community organizers and local politicians. But the art and the poetry has always been at the core of his actions. As a result, Papoleto has produced and participated in a multitude of programs and readings with not only poets, but with musicians, dancers and visual artists. If that wasn't enough, every January 6, Papoleto dons brocade robes and a glittering crown to assume his annual role as King Emeritus for Three Kings Day, *El Día de Los Reyes Magos,* to celebrate his culture, his community, and his own being. Activism is not only talking about or writing about the issues you care about. Sometimes you have to break down barriers, and go beyond the mind and the book. You carry a sign into the street. You feed the poor. You celebrate with your community. You welcome new people into your community. You break down the walls.

The way we see it, Papoleto is a countercultural wanderer who uses the power of words to send messages to the masses, to remind us of our history and our humanity. He participates in and then records these events with poetic fervor, always remaining faithful to his edict, that a true poet is a literary activist, and is a vital necessity of life.

All of this is evident in PAPOLíTICO. As Papoleto uses poetry to pinpoint the hypocrisy of this country, and challenge the status quo, he does so in simplistic yet ironic terms: "This is a free country! / Oh… *(How much is that freedom / in the window?!)*" ("Mediocrysis" p. 15). In his poem, "To Pay a National Debt—to Puerto Rico, Oscar Lopez Rivera Must be Set Free Immediately!" he addresses the movement to free this Puerto Rican political prisoner, as well as condemning the growing loss of local control and the newly imposed debtor status, while reminding readers of the radioactive residue that still remains, not just on Vieques, but throughout the island of Puerto Rico: "Where now radioactive beachfront condominiums & bungalows / are being sold to the sons of bitches & daughters of the newly riché, / Who *Bill* the exploited on *Our Madre Isla* for the cost incurred / for the exploitation of the Nation we no longer own!" (p. 113).

Papoleto's work tweaks classic poetry, creating new metaphors that resonate with classic poetic expressions. For example, British poet William Blake's bird was a prisoner in "Song: How sweet I roam'd from field to field," "He caught me in his silken net, / And shut me in his golden cage," Papoleto's bird is entombed within a commercial message in "Mediocrysis" (p.15):

> "Here flies the Sweet Bird of Liberty
>     on the box
>         of a brand New Product …
>     Now you see it,
>             *Now you don't—*
>     Now it's On Sale,
>             *Now it's at Regular Price!*"

(p. 20)

The beauty of Papoleto's poetry is that he refuses to be remained trapped into a singular ideal or language. While others have labelled him solely as a Nuyorican poet, Papoleto sees himself as an "American poet" who happens to be an Afro-Puerto Rican and sees the world from a Nuyorican perspective. He is a poet that has an appreciation of William Blake, Ezra Pound and Walt Whitman, in addition to Langston Hughes, Amiri Baraka, Sonia Sanchez, Julia de Burgos, Tato Laviera and Pedro Pietri.

Written in the "cascading" style that dictates the beat and rhythm of his poems, Papoleto investigates the serious and mundane with the satirical and ironic wit he has become known for as he expresses his frustration with the harsh realities we live in today.

Finally, not all of the poems are about political messaging. It is perhaps one of the reasons we love "Baseball Fever" (p. 62). It doesn't tackle any particular social issue; it is a poem that is whimsical and fun:

> "After His Team!
>> (for which he does not
>>> play
>> , nor have otherwise
>>> a say
>> but is fanatically
>>> in love
>> with them)
>>> Just winning
>>> *The World Series!*"

This poem personally reminds us of our annual Fourth of July softball game in Woodstock, and of Papoleto's love for the game. With consummate athletic skill, in 2013, Papoleto executed perhaps the most memorable single event of twenty-two years of the softball games — an unassisted triple play: Papoleto was positioned at first base, with runners on first and second, and no outs. He caught a line-drive at first base, tagged the base, then threw to the ball to the Short Stop for the forced out at second base; scored: 3-3-3-6 as a play. Complete joy!

It's inclusion in PAPOLíTICO serves to remind readers that despite the uphill battles we face as a nation, there are moments of joy that get us through our daily challenges, and allows light in to illuminate the shadows. Joy helps heal wounds, and fills our souls with goodness. This essential ingredient of joy is found in many of his poems, even in some of the poems that challenge societal ills.

Enjoy and cherish the righteous poems in PAPOLíTICO. Papoleto's cries for justice are sorely needed these days. We can draw solace from the fact that poets such as Papoleto are around to remind and inspire us, to offer solace and, at the same time, make us think a little more deeply about what's happening in the world today. ❖

—Joel Kovel and DeeDee Halleck

# INDENTURED

In
  The United Stat(E)
       of America,
  an old
    Black man
     in 21st Century,
     125th Street,
        Harlem,
   with a
      broom
       &
      dust pan
   in his hands,
        cursing
         while chasing
      this empty
         bag
      of potato
       chips,
      twirling
       round
      on the
       sidewalk
      in this
       circle

         , blame
     the wind.

# A COP HAIKU

Group of Cops,
   buying
         *Coquitos*;
Different *Flavors,*
*Different* Cops!

# HUMAN WISDOM

It is important
        to keep
           culture,
Culture is The Essence
                of Life;
   It's life itself . . .

The Story of Peoples'
            ways—
  How they made
    their way
        in Life,
to deal with life,
     to understand it,
       Their understanding
      cultivated
         in
    this wisdom,
  passed on
       through
          children
            for Ever.

Their ancient cries,
        the moans
    of Living
      Souls,

                    reLiving
              a past,
              a part
        a being of
                themselves,

        removed

        & yet contained
                        within
                itself.

  Some People lay
                eXtinct,
          their way
                  unknown;
        The Sum
                of their
                        eXistence
              as erased
              as footsteps
                      in the sand;

  Some People are
                  as dead
            as dead
                  can be
                      dead;
          Their memory
                (the memory
                      of them) …

disappeared
from memory
itself—

No one left of it
to speak for it—
Not a soul
alive
to weep for its dead,
Its Sacrifice …

This,
That wells within the breasts
of Women,
in the Womb
itself;
in the water
where Sperm
swims,

— Innate,
this wisdom

… Like the cool
& demure Flower
forcing its way
through Earth
to the light of
Day;
To see the Sun!

To place its blooming Face
before it!
To be rooted
in this unKnown
place
, to which
We give a foreign Name
as meaning just the Same
Wherever we
are standing
— There,
Celebrating!
The DistinCtive
Cultures
of a man
, which
make us
common men.

# MEDIOCRYSIS

*(for my friend, Dylcia Pagan)*

There Are No Political Prisoners,
    in the United States of AmericA!...

This is a free country!
               *Oh... (How much is that freedom*
                       *in the window?!)*

   As long as
       the Supermarket shelves
              are full,
  The People fool themselves
     to thinking
         Everything's
            just fine!...

*Though nothing is*
     *really free;*
  Everything costs Some*thing*
        & *Some*Things cost
              more than
                  others
       & *Other*s are worth
        far less
         than what you pay
            for them!—
    Yeah, Everybody knows this
          & more

, but they still ignore
            The price tag
                on the semblance of the freedom
                                    they adore!
    Therefore,
        There Are No Political Prisoners,
            in the United States of AmericA!...

    Everybody who's in jail
        was a Criminal at Large!
                            — Guilty as they're Charged!
        (Every single one of them
            is Arrested proportionately
            to their numbers in society,
        Though they're still
            in the minority, They are free
                                to Commit
        The vast majority of crimes
            Against Society
                    & Therefore
                CONstitute
                    the so-accused & jailed majority
                                of the minority.)

    These criminals,
            through their own hand,
        All broke some Law of this Land!...
        Contemptuous & Seditious —
            Though they may believe( each one of them, alone
                in their own separate cells) in their own
                kind of God,

They are criminals, nevertheless—
To wit, They must Concede
                        While we refuse to Confess...


So that *Everytime*
            You see THE POLICE having their way
                              with someOne of us,
        Apprehended in their custody
                Thrown up against
                              a building,
            Or their face
                    against the pavement...
You *just* walk on by
            assUming that the Culprit
                              is Guilty
                    of some Crime,
        say   , *Even* if
                        it's for possession
                    of a dime-bag
                              of weed,
                *( ... 'though Racism*
            *is still Not Against the Law!*
                *— Not even for those*
                    *paid to uphold the Law!*
        *Nor are Biased Crimes*
            *"A Thing of the Past!"*
            *in these,*
                *The most modernist of times!)*


Still the ghetto-man/child
                *needs to be Corrected*

through the System of
THE REMEDIAL RELIGIOUS INSTRUCTIONS
OF THE DEPARTMENT OF CORRECTIONS
INSTITUTIONAL HIGH SCHOOL FOR
THE ADVANCEMENT OF PETTY CRIMES
TO HIGH MISDEMEANORS in the Hub of
149th Street & St. Ann's Avenue
in the South South Bronx!

Though the Youths' Social needs
                                    Go otherwise neglected,
            They stand, nonetheless, Convicted
            of what shouldn't even be a crime;
            Was not once upon a time, is now
                                    forevermore
                        Firing up a Blunt(
                        *As is your whole culture)*
                                    — Up/Against the Law!!!…
            *While the more Freedom You have,*
                                    *The less Liberty is Yours!*

You can't even look up to Contemporary Adults—
Who, with some vague sense of cultural intellect
and lack of self respect, stand on their knees
with their arms outstretched, placated
by the mediocrity of democracy
they embrace in the jobs they hold, or hold not.
Locked-up into their System of Circumstance,
Content with their Lottery in Life.
Living in a state of Quasi-fear,
Aspiring to be absorbed by the dysfunctional

social order that governs here;
Believing every word told onto them —
About what they can and cannot do;
What they can become —
                              Despite where they come from!
Because, for them, there is *No Cause* worth dying for;
No country held captive by this one or that to fight for;
No injustice unjustly persecuting — No one to protest for!
For, as far as they believe, *They Believe*
They are as "American" as Americans are unconcerned,
Misinformed about the vast wasteland of their Imperial Empire
Where no one citizen can use a piece of toilet tissue
to wipe their butts without oppressing someone, somewhere
in this world.
   Left blindly wondering what they should think,
      Independently and otherwise,
   Than the facts disguised before their eyes,
      focused on the thin, obscured consumer line
         that moves ever further & further away
            from the plainness of Truth
                              , blurred
               & as elusive as the sands of time
    That, in time, becomes
      The writing on the wall,
         that you convince yourself to believe …

      *While the more you look around you
         the less Freedom you have to throw away!*

Yo!
    Here flies the Sweet Bird of Liberty
     on the box
       of a brand New Product ...
    Now you see it,
         *Now you don't—*
    Now it's On Sale,
         *Now it's at Regular Price!*

   O, We have nothing to fear
            but Paranoia itself—
  'Cause
    No, There are no Political Prisoners
              here...

# STORY FROM A MOUNTAIN

Palm Trees…
       *Long,*
          And slenderswaying…
                  Palm Trees!

                    …like
Brownfinned Mermaids
        of Earth, Green
              eyes     Danced!
   in the sun setting breeze,
          Moist
             with this ancient sea
                 that enfolds us,
  Spilling its
      OceanfloorJewels
          wet
           into the cup of our nets…

And this,
  like
    The Waves that come to tumble,  soft
                 on our sand
  O!, Drew the ships to our shores
         And,the horses
         And,the armored men
         And,their chains!

                    CHRISTIAN SOLDIERS
                    THEY CALLED THEMSELVES
                                        GODS!!!

...with Flags & Guns
     in Helmets of Steel,
               THEY came
                    with their Swords Drawn!!!
                                   ...against our offering
               of Dancers!:
                    Earth Beings
                         —*Flying in the night*
                                        —Flying
                    through Fire
                         like Stars
                                   ...smokelessly!!!


Our Fruits
          ,soft
               with their rainbow color
                         (so like the laughter
                              that once came to *these* children)
     , Unaware
          *THE WAR!*
     were Crushed
          beneath the Weight
               of Marching Boots...


                    And their Swords!
                         — so Much,

Their *"God of Thunder!"*
Fell heavy
on our Homes.

Hugged
With their final Mother's smiles,
*THE CHILDREN*
were Murdered!
: Caoyuca!
Ponce!
Sierra Maestra!
Algiers!

O!, Pass your hand, tenderly
Over this body that bleeds…
*MYLAI*
& this swollen eye—
That
…is *Wounded Knee.*

# FOR THE ANGEL DIAZES

Who has pity for Angel Diaz?
Who pities he who killed a cop,
So accused till proven guilty
though otherwise innocently presumed;
Who took the life of a new york city
police officer (one of its finest—
a husband, a father, a man
of a family who loved; a home
where love abode)
Who murdered him in the coldest blood,
Who took his life in the prime of his life —
Who lost his own in the prime of his own lost life?

For what was he, but a lost *Soul* on Earth
Who wrote of himself in his prison cell,
  *"I have no worth. My life is shit.*
   *I want to diediedie..."*

     (one death, being enough
                       for
                          the living)

    & thus
      He did,
           Thus he did,
                thus he did...

At the hands of *his* hands — Hanged by himself

So say *They* who were there, but did not help.
Hanged by a belt, without doubt
　　American-Made by American's *hands*.

That nothing else remains of him
　　but his mother's lonely tears for him,
　　　& the memory of his sin;
Who cries for the child, to whom
　　She gave birth
　　　And now buries in the same dirt of Earth
　　　　as lay he whom her son killed.

Yea! We weep openly for the death of the cop
But not for the death of the crook,
Whose life was wasted as *just* the same;
Society accepting none of the blame
　　for the pain of his life,
Nor excuses him itself for not saving his soul —
　　As if he were bad from the womb,
　　As if he remains bad in his tomb!...

　　　For
　　　　ReVenGe's sake—
　　　Justice was not served!

And the wailing mouths of babes
　　go yet unfilled by food or hope,
And another youth grows to claim his own
　　way to live his life
And name him *Angel,* or even *Jesús*

And see what becomes the plot of his lot.
'Lest blame & fault fall equally upon the same line
   that distinguishes, then dismisses
      in the same breath;

Mothers kill their children,
Fathers let their newborn sons die of hunger, while
Social Service agencies turn the other cheek;
   as if to see if the social view is better elsewhere
      where there might be a different need.
And all the while, it's greed that feeds
   at this banquet of human famine.

# SUBWAY SLEEPER CAR SLEEPER

Sometimes, *Someone's* life
                              just
         *falls* right down;
                  (and so,
                     one needs to take a nap)
                                    in Life...


: Man on subway train
                    sleeping
           across four seats
                       in the corner,
            on the *Morning*
                      rush-hour train
                             to work...


    His combat-construction, worker-type
                                  boots
                       stretched out
                             to the very end
                                       of
                       the row of seats,
                                    So as
                    no one else
                        can sit there
                               beside him,
                                    spider
                          or human
                                or not.

It's 9 o'clock
          in the *Morning,*
     and he looks like
          he's been sleeping there
                    for hours,
                         perhaps
               throughout
                    the entire *Night* . . .

His head pillowed
     by a see-through plastic bag,
                    looks like
          a garbage bag
               full of stuff (
                    not of dreams)
                         Now
          all that's left
               that belongs to him;

and his winter-Parka
          all buttoned-up
                    tight
          to keep him warm,
     and his left hand
          in his jeans' pocket (
                    perhaps
          protecting a wallet
          of loosely held
                    change)
     and his left knee

just slightly
benT
for his comfort's
sake—
...On his commute
(unlike
wine to Vermouth)
As the train
fills up
with more passengers
passing by
on their ways
to work;

Having *Awaken!*
Showered
Shaved
& Shitted,
*Breakfasted*
or not,
nevertheless
Got up
from their beds,
Got dressed
& left
their humble abodes,
walked out
into the blistering cold,
& are now
left standing
frigidly

in aisles
against
the opening
& closing of doors,
looking for
the promised seat
that they,
this *Morning*
having slipped through
their *MetroCards,*
Thus they paid for
& had hoped
so desperately for
*the Seat*
that is no more
a seat
to sit upon,
but for the homeless
to *Sleep*.

# AGAINST THE THREAT OF AIDS

*(for so many friends, and my brother Tito)*

Death Discriminates Not,
                    Against The Living!
    :Death Kills All Living Things!
        Death Kills Your Life!
                    IT, ends, IT
                            :HERE
                                    , on this Earth
                                        as(wE KnoW
                                                of)IT!
                                            That's It!


But Disease!... O! But Disease Discriminates,
                            Disease is Selective
                                        of Its Victims:

    Some Are Children
                    , Whose eyes have yet to wander
                                    through their lives
            Who we've seen before
                        starving to their deaths
                                at the floor
                                    of our dinner tables
                                                :!Bombed Upon—
                                            Burned!
                                    Broken Dolls;
                                        Massacred!
                                            Mass Murdered!
                    Crying with their open mouths...

Unheard above the dancing crowds!...
Old Men!
            , After their lives;
                    Their children&their wives
                                    their affairs,
              their cars&cares
                        Die,
        wrinkled
            among the unknown sheets
                        of strange hospital beds
                                    , No One
                            not even
                                    the shadows of their wives
                                    showing their heads.


On Colorful Posters,
                Children
                    , unable to take a playful step
                                    into this world
                        without the aid
                                    of the iron-exoskeletons
                        into which they were born,
        elicit our poor sympathy  (unlike
                        The Attitude Assumed Against
                                        This illicit misery
                                which now
                                    lay its peril
                                        Across
                            the whole of society)!
        ...O! Our tears are endless
                        for the litheless,

reaching the depths
        of our wallets,
             where wallow our hearts
                lost
             in deep debt
*"To Give Support!"*
        …as we so poorly know how.


How Is It?!... THEN!!!
      That so many of my Friends
       Have come to meet their End
       Without Even,
          the Government
       A Relative
        or Friend
          There!
     , at that last moment
          in their lives
   To let a tear come to their eyes,
    To send a friend
       a kiss Goodbye,
         a hug
    Or give a reason why?!…
Young men, in their prime
      Die,
        as old wrinkled men aged with time;
     From the moment of their first breath
             , Babies born
             doomed to their death;
While Junkies
    , still in ghetto streets

                              nod & leap from window sills
                                        in one
                                      last
                                          wasted haste
                                  to leave this hell
                                    they've lived to hate!!!…

…in this Society
          , where all that melts into its pot
                    comes out asplasticpiecesofshit
                              thatRepresent,IT
          Having Lovers, making love like this:
                              with plastic tubes
                                    between their bliss
                                                  , unsure
                                        of ThemSelves
                                                  , embraced
                                                  in True Love
                                    wearing surgical gloves!


Why Is It?!… THAT!!!
                    This Disease
                        which kills with such great ease
                    goes on
                              , unnoticed
                                  as if a subtle breeze?!


Could it be, That Our Great Society
                        has Acquired
                        an acute Immunity to the needs of its
                                                  own community,
                    a Deficiency in humanity;

a sickly Syndrome of insanity!

Why else would IT  go ignored

by Those

Whom we implore

to convene

on the floor of Humanity

And allow Science to explore

an End

to this Dread Disease

—Instead of mixing Bombs

with eyes designed against You&Me!


I can only wonder:

…"How lonely Death must be?"

… any Death must be!

, a lonely destiny

Reserved

for Every

Living Being!

O! But To Go!!!…O! BUT TO GO!!!!!….

Through the Door of Life's Great Mystery

, unblessed by Society

, unlike a Soldier

, without Regality

now

Scum,

now Filth,

Diseased

Debris!

This...
This...
, said of a fellow
Human Being!

I do not think of my Friends, like this
To me, *They* are Beautiful;
my Friends! my Family!
*My Brothers & Sisters*
*of Mother Earth:*
THEIR DEATH WAS NOT THEIR FAULT!!!
NOOO!!!!!!
*You cannot blame their Deaths*
*on Them!*
My Friends, as Yours,
tried to live their lives
*as Full*
*as the Brightness*
*in their Eyes!*
—THAT IS WHAT EVERYONE TRIES!

My Eyes will meet Their Eyes
in the bright glaze of Another Sky!
We will be Friends again,
*My Friends,*
And We Will Be Whole,
without
disease,
...Far Far!!!
, from this Society's Hypocrisy!

# TOURISM UP + DOW/JONES, 6PTS.

WELCOME TO SAN DIEGO!
(Now Go Home!!!)        Say
        theBumperstickers     , Last Stop
                        in the u.s.
                                of.a.

    Where
        the driving civilian population
                            has the freeway
            To run over Mexican
                        Illegal
                        Aliens
                            on the HighWay,    All
                            on the Run
                                trying to escape
                                    their native tongue
            To find a decent job
                in a land
                    where they
                        can't speak
                            a Word
                        of the
                            langua(gj)e
                                The People
                                    use there
                        to abuse Them;
                                I've seen Them:

        Lying dead
            On the sides of the road;

The road to Mexico,
The road to San Diego...
wrappped in blankets
of finer cloths
than the rags of their own clothes;
It is this way,
*It is this way...*

These UnNumBereD
OutNumBereD
OutLaWeD
Hard Workers
Become DoCuMenTeD
Dead People
in the morgue
of a strange world,
truly forgotten.

# SUICIDALSOCIETALITY

THE MAN *from* THE UNITED STATES IMMIGRATION OFFICE
                                                                    drives

   an unmarked
        VEHICLE (which does not say so)
  slowly
     through the streets
        of sunny San Diego
          like
    a catcher of stray dogs,
        looking for
         *People*
        who *are*
   so described by *THE AUTHORITIES* (
        on said subject matter)(
  *To Whom* such a thing
      would matter) of *These*
         pretentiously un-
           united states
             of human conflict
         of what is LEGAL,&
         what is FAIR,&
          jUST, what is Just?—
Ice!,  Describes these people's feelings
  with whose lips they kiss their wives,
       *"GoodMorning!"*
         & go off
  To Do, THE DUTY they must DO
     as *THE HOLY*

and *UNLAWFUL*
so prescribe, So....
They spend this day chasinG(&)CatchinGrown
MEN
*in the Image of GOD*
, Whom(
They say
)They represent.


It was one clear and sunny such San Diego day,
*My Eyes*
with me behind them,
had the sad misfortune
TO WITNESS UNTO GOD!
(It was not a lovely sight!
No, Not one!)
One would not have wanted to see it for oneself:


*THEIR VEHICLE* was stopped at the corner of an indecent street
where crimes of daily indiscreet agree to meet, to transact life
with a sad and mundane fact,
waiTing...
for the light to change,
like a patient vehicle of unsuspecting
unImportance,
eXcept for the lives of its occupants(
all living in a slow, kind
of
hurry...
)WHEN!

ALL-OF-A-MEAN, ALL-OF-A-SUDDEN!

               *...THE SIDE DOOR FLIES OPEN!!!*

AND OUT RUNS THIS MAN—AT THE TOP OF HIS DESPERATE HEART'S SPEED!!!...

                                 Like

                                  a Kid !

  ...just doing *SomeThing,* & he has to Run to do it!

                  WHEN / THEN!!!!!!...

TWO OTHER GROWN MEN — JUMP OUT OF THE VEHICLE VAN

  & GIVE CHASE TO THE MAN, *Down the street*—

                 Just like Kids!!

  ...having done *SomeThing*—& just have to Run!!!

               WHEN!!!

                  ONE MAN dives through the air...

O, This is Tense —Not at all —Not at ease!

         And HE tackles *the Man,* Running

          like WE love to see in the Movies!

                  But This Is Not!

This is *Real,*

     *Life* unfolding in a Drama!...

  And HE knocks *Him* down to the ground—

          *His face* against the ground

           like the sole of a very determined shoe

                    , instead

        *A Man* and His Soul *against* the ground!

There is a terrible Fight!

       :You really don't want to see It! (Unless,

             of Course,

    You enjoy such sights, find in them

           some delight

      As a poet might be

         condemned to do)

TWO GROWN MEN FIGHTING!!!
TWO GROWN MEN with their *hands* rolled into *FISTS!!!*
THROWING *THEIR FISTS* against *the Sea of Air* (

                    striking *Angels!*   & *Demons!*
                       *the Wind!*
                            *the Breath of Life!...* )

  Trying *desperately* TO KILL!!!
                    *Each Other* off,
     *Full* of HATE against *Each Other*—
                   For *Un*Known Reasons
                         In This World?!
                   *Un*Known To *Them!*
                  Un*Known* To You!
                          Certainly
                           A Mystery to me!


WHEN / THEN!!!— THE OTHER GROWN MAN Jumps in
                (And HE'S against *the Man*
                      who started it
                      with *His Running*)
  And, very quickly *(in the heat of this day)*
                  — It's all over between THEM!


Together now, THE MEN drag *the Man* away, like heavy
                *L*
                *U*
                *G*
                *G*
                *A*
                *G*
                *E*

And, THEY throw *Him* among
*the Other Men,*
Whom
THEY'VE betrayed as *Men*
ON THIS GOD-GIVEN DAY!!!....

*WWWWWWWEEEEEEEEEEEEEEEEEEEEEEEELLLLLLLLLLLLLLLLLLLLLL!!!!!!!*
*EEEEEEEEEEEEELLLLLLLLLLLLLLLLLLLLLLLLLLLLLLLLLLLLLLLLLLLL!!!!!!!!!!!!!!*

I—FIND—MYSELF—WITH—MY—THROAT—FILLED!!!
WITH—MY—OWN—BLOOD—
YELLING:
*LET HIM GOOOOOOOO!!!!!!*
*MOTHERFUUUCCCCCCCKKKK*
*EERRRR ERE RRRSS!!!RS*
*LET HIM GOOOO !!!! OOOOOHH HHOOHHHO*
*OOHHOOOOOHH HH!!!!!!!!!...*

And Peo*Ple*
, milling around in their circles
in the street
below
Look uP to my window—
*in their eYes*
*i could see thEm,*
*thinking;*
"I AM
MAD!!!"

# A CONVERSATION WITH A BLIND MAN

*(for Kevin)*

I have no idea
             ,What
         caused HiS
     Blindness,
                 If he was born
                             like that
    I did not dare
                 to ask,
          thinking it
                     rude
          to inquire
                     How Life
                         had been so
                                 cruel
                                     ,or perhaps
                                         that He
                 was just as well
                         without his eyes
                                     ...Still
     all, that He could see
         is in his
                 Mind...
                     And i,
                 could
                     not help
                             but, wondered
                                     whY

He could never see
                ,This Scene
                    just passed my eyes:
                                    i  t    bi    t
                                ty      ty
                                        flowErBLOS
                                        SOMS
                                    sleeping
                                        inab
                                        unch
                                &a regular,
                                        old
                                            pesky
                                    housefly
                                        LanDs
                                                so
                                                ex
                                                ac
                                                TI
                                                    y
                                                on
                                            just
                                        one
    Nor,
        The Early
                Mourning
            puffed-up
                    faces
                of waking bums—
        As if
            in their sleeps,

Their dreams
had beat
them up;
Their, Shopping Carts
of Life's belongings
/lined up
like Vehicles
against the curb
as Homeless
Men&Women
,now appearing
in
the workday
Light
like dirt
tumBling
oVer
,Awake
from their
Policedisturbed slumber
on the grassy
knolls
of private,
Urban
front/Yards
Sprawled
with bro
k
en
card
board

                                                    box
                                                        es
                                            upon which
                                                        recline
                                        the destitute
                                                        ,waiting
                                        their turn
                                                    to die.

I ask, My Foolish Self
                        ,the (?) *"Why"*
        My Mind
                not believing
                        its
                        own eyes
                                —Though
                        they've
                                no History
                                        of telling lies
                                                As they look
                                                        ,across
                                        the whole
                                                of Society
                                                        ,searching for     *the Beauty*
                                        ,confounded by
                                                Futility....

        (taxi cab
                prospective
                        drivers
                                &FBI agents
                        ,line up

to get

their cabs

for the

day

—Hoping

for

the best

of the fleet

—to Hustle

un

fair

fares

from strangers

,visitors;

citizens

yet, foreigners

to the unTold

Penal

Code

of this city's

unswept

streets)

He told me

he played Piano

,that Jazz

was the Music

he Loved

,but/Hated

playing in chic

smoke-filled

clubs

,where the lovers
              of jaZZ
   & all that Stuff
       would mispronounce
          their favorite
                  drinks
                      ,till they
          could no longer
             use their minds
          to think
       &blow
          their cigarettes
                   into his eyes
                       —forcing them
          to blinK.

O! The Sun Is Bright!
              /Against Any Eyes
                      —Opening
          ...to Live
                  ,yet another
                  Day!
   But in the streets
          ,where ,Nothing
                      gets
          a good night's sleep
                      —Its Light Explodes!
                              in
                  blanked-out Irises
                          ,Once
   flickered, by childish lash

es,
　—Now
　　　all too-much/Accustomed/to
　　the daily whips&lashes
　　　　　　,Reality un
　　leashes, beginning with the lies
　　　　　spitted from the mouths of politician'sSpeeches
　　　　　　　　　　　　　　　FOR THEY ARE
　　　　　　　　　　　　　　　　　THE TRUE
　　　　　　　　　　　　　　LEECHES
　　　　　　　　　　　　　　　　of

　　　　　Life's pure Treasures
　　　　　　　,earning SO MUCH
　　　　for doing notmuch at all
　　　　　　　　with Great Pleasure;
　　　　　　　　　　leaving, thePoor
　　　　　　　　　　　　so more
　　　　　　　　　　　　poorly
　　　　　　　　　　　　　confused
　　　　　　　　　　　　　　　:to
　　　　　　　　measure out, the rest of their lives
　　　　　　　with dull plastic spoons
　　　　　　　　　　,Howling
　　　　　　　　　　　like Dogs
　　　　　　　at their lives' FullMoon
　　　　　　　　　　　　,gone!...

Perhaps,
　　My Friend
　　　　is blind
　　　　　by Choice

                    ,HiS OwN!
        refusing(
              to see) anymore;
                          He's locked
              his mind's door
                          /Against the face
                                of a society
                                      of hoards
                    Who have
                          ,EveryThing
                    that
                          Money could possibly buy
                                            ,&Still
                          are bored, unconscious
                                            of
                          their leisured lives
                                      ,while somebody like me
        is forced
          to see 'TheM' daily
                    ,flaunting
                          their Fancy Autos
                                ,to GasUp
                                      &Go
                    complain
                    about a
                          drop
                    of rain
                          ,on a terrain
                                where
                    it never snows(
                          hidden kept

)Their treasured pain.

O! Tourists Come, &
                Tourists Go
                        ,seeing less
                            of what truly goes
                                        beneath
                                            their open nose
                        ,Conscientiously
                                rejecTing    *"Those"*
                        conDemned, unSightly
                                        by    *"ThOSE"*
                            if only, sLightly(
                                    Above
                                        the spit)
                                            be
                        neath
                            their own feet
                                    ,Where these sad souls
                                            are consoled
                                                in sleep.


ON THIS DAY!
    In The BrightBroadLight
                        ,in plainSight(
                                sublime)
        only to the blind:
                Shoppers will die
                    on the lines
                        that they keep
                                ,Born
                                    to Shop

too wallet-proud
                to weep
                        —Buying, yeT
        ANother
        ComPuTeR
                —This One,
                        proMising
        to do MoRe
                than
                the One
                        before—
                        Until next
                                week
                                        ,When
        a brand-new Shopper's born;
                                Human Aliens

will ,Still
        illegally
                /Cross
                        im   a
                        g in   a
                                ry
                                        bo
                                rde
                                        rs
                                        ,as birds
                                        & bugs
                                        fly freely
                                                to &
                                                fro
                        from Mexico

                                        to
                              San Diego;
                                        While Negroes

          ,in the Black Night
                         of Life
          rob MoM&PoP
                    ,corner grocery
                              stores
                                   runNing through
                                        smashed open doors
                                                  with nothing
                                                       more
                              than useless papers
                                        in their hands;
                                                  Their Shadows

               still hovering
                         in Slavery,
                                   leaving Death
               where They
                         now stand:
                                   And,
                              Young Girls' Dreams

               go, up in smoke
     in the heat of a stranger's
                    AnGRyPAsSIoN'SRaGE!
          passing this, as if some gift
                         ,Confusing Hate!
                                   for Human Bliss!...
                                             While, Tomorrow

          ,a new
          Born

baby
        CRiiiES!!!...
    for
        SomeThing
            as yet, UnKnown
                    to Humankind!...
How Can The World
        Be Like This!?
                    ...so, Cruel!
                            & yet,
        It still is Life!...
                    ...OHNO!!!
                    HE DID NOT SAY
                            what He had seen
                                    ,Although

I could feel
        HiS feeling's feelings, seeping through
                    this blinded Human Being
                                Even, He
                                Could See

    :Life is Nothing, but DeMeaning
                        —Void
        of its own
                feeling,
                        unyielding
        in its cruelty
                toward, the so many human bleeding!...


                            ...O! Blind Men!

                            ...O! Blind Men!

We'll always see
                theM
                        ,standing
                                with their
                                        sticks
                at
                Bus Stops
                                ...waiting
                wondering
                                (through
                        their black
                                eyes)   ,Perhaps
        "What Bus
                is This?!"

# UNITY SPEAK...

The sad condition
   of powerless people,
           looking into the face
  of the Mighty
        & Powerful
with frail, blinking eyes —
as if a wisp of dust
     continuously passes before them...

Their voice as cracked as sun-baked skin;
Their yell, a whimper in the vacuumed ear
   of the un-disconcerted many

 Trying desperately
        to *Become*
           a *Cell*...
  in the intestinal tissue
   of the monster
    that's swallowed them.

# BASEBALL FEVER

This,
   Black *Cat,*
      with an *Angels'*
        baseball cap
           on
             his head
        , in Boston
      holds his index finger
           up in the air
     in the face
       of the wandering camera,
                Man!
   After *His* Team!
       (for which he does not
            play
      , nor have otherwise
           a say
       but is fanatically
            in love
       with them)
           Just winning
            *The World Series!*

         smiling
          without a tooth
            in his mouth
              , he says
                *"We're #1!"*

# THE MILLION YOUTH MARCH #1

The concert ends at Exactly 9 o'clock
Yet the entitled couples linger in Central Park
　　way past midnight,
　　　　mesmerized by the silent eyes
　　　　　of the full moon against the blackened sky…

But *The Million Youth March*
Must end emphatically an hour past 3
　　in the afternoon
Because this is a society,
　　the majority afraid of the minority,
Untrusting of its youth
Though its future,
　　　　　　　　they love it say,
　　　　　　　　　is entirely in its own hands…

Although this is a holiday weekend, and
There's no school till Tuesday morning,
This police state of denial( Part&Parcel to
　　the dysfunctional denial
That mistrusts itself for lack of faith;
That instructs one to turn the other cheek
While no one better lay a hand on it, the Other),
While *They* are being beat in all the Negro streets
Not shown on any T.V. News,
Not sharing views contrary to the status
　　of the Statue Quo,
Programmed into thinking its belief
is its own innocence.

# BEAT WHITE DUDE

White Dude
    gets beat
        buying drugs from a BlacX duDe
        on the corner of
            5th & Market Street,
             San Diego
        (anywhere, really)
               Why else
                would a

White boy
    give money
     to a black guy
        in the middle
       of a friday night
         in the street?
               — Because he loves
                    him(?)
I hear the white boy yell,
      "call the Police!!!
      call the Police!!!"
        He's been offended
              , it's obvious
      But he ain't defending his right
              , he's just yelling
                 — a baby
        does the
         same thing with tears
          & accomplishes more.

The Black dude goes
           of course,
                running in the night,
                      with the flash
            of the white dude
                in hot pursuit...

I play it cool
        , go shoot some pool
              across the street
         in a bar,
           a bar where Black
                people
         go drink & listen to
                oldies
         , converse
           play pool
                , away from
           the rest
            of the world.

I'm playing by myself now
        and can't seem to win;
    The White Ball seems
           to follow the eight ball    into
              the pocket
      all the fucking time!

The Police come, in 2 girls & a guy cop...
    They look silly & out of place,
           but they're there.

They start searching the bathroom,
        like all of them
          need
            to go at once;
They look under the tables,
      lift glasses
        & all    go in the back &
    look in the *Frig*...

The respectable,
    Black
      businessman proprietor
         *Questions*
           their *Act*—
      *"This is My Place of*
        *Business...*"
           "WE'RE DOING OUR BUSINESS,"
           is bitterly shot back!

The beat white dude
      stands in the shadows of
         our stare.

He's called the
      Police;
        They are looking for a black Dude,
        anyone will do,
'Cause the white boy
      got beat
        copping drugs on 5th
         & Market Street.

# DRAMA ON T.V.

*Amer*-I-cans!!!...
    *(These*
        *Sissies of*
          *no*-Emotion): Made in the U.S.A.
                           , say
                             the labels
                                   on
                           EVERY
                           THING
                               made
                       SomeWhere
                               else
                            no less
                            for less
                               by SomeOne
                            else
                         paid less
                              than
                               made in the U.S.A.
                                     , say

When
  A *Tragedy*
    occurs on T.V.
           ,where *All* is *Nothing*
             but pure fantasy
                  , a COMMERCIAL comes on
            almost IMMEDIATELY

Selling US someThing
, sooThing
whatever sTings
, diverTing
our feeLings
from
the spans      of our aTt*en*
tions.
…Can't Stand to let you,
*po*   n   d*er*
THE PAIN
you've just seen,
Even If
it's unREAL.


GEORGE
*shoots*
LENNIE
in*"Mice&Men"*
on(T.V.)
*in the back*
*of the*
*head…*   The perFect BLT;
Mayonaise bUy
BEST FOODS


When *the Drama*
*reSumes…* (
we have forgotten

what had happened
, although
there is a human body
*lying* dead
on the ground

), But we can *smell*
*the* Bacon!
siZZling on the pan!

# A SAN DIEGO SOUTHERN/AFRICAN NIGHT

(O i have no opinion
            *of What My Eyes See!...*)


:There's a black man,
            A man whose skin is black
                        — the color,
                                    BlacK!

    Running across The Street
        in the middle of the night;
                    BlacK NighT!
                        Only the flickering lights of business buildings
                                                        ,still
                        burning in the night(
                                    like the eyes
                                    of obese monsters)
                    And the stars,
                            of course   —They
                                        in their distance
                    are out tonight;
                            Quietly knowing,
                            Unsaying a word.


THE TRAFFIC LIGHT CHaNGeS —
    So Now, The Color RED is Against
                        HiM—WHO crosses The Street!
                                    POLICECAR
                                    cruises   by... And

                                        SeiZe HiM!
                                                (BlackMan)
                                        & FLaSHeS
                                        itS LiGHtS
                                                BRiiiiGhHtTtT!!!!!!!!

¡¡¡In the Middle of the Night
RED&OrANGe/BlUe&WHiTE!!!
LiGHTS!!!!!!!!!!!!!!!!!!!!!!!!!!!!!!!!!!!!!!!!!!!!!!!!!!!!!!!!!!!!!!!!!!!!!!!!!!!!!!!!!!!!!!!!!!!!!!!!!!!!!!!!!!!!!!!!!!
                                        THEY cut HiM off at the pass
                                        Of the corner of a sidewalk/UP
                                                        Against!
                                        TheCARRRR!!!MOTHER!!!!!!!!


HiS Hands on the hood
    He is forced to spread his legs A/ParTWIdE— Like this
                                        THEY Dare call it Eagle!
        So THEY could search him up good, To make sure
                                There's nothing up his sleeve
                                The/re/s/no/thi/ng/u/p/hi/S/m/i……n/D!
            :THEY take his wallet ,from out of him/
                                Removing the papers   ,from the person
            :THEY tell him to go sit in the car/
                                In the memory of the back seat,
                                    Looking out the window like that, perhaps
                                                    resembling a bird


And He obeys THEM,
            HE does
    What HE believes that THEY say/
                                It is dead night.
                                The night is dead.

                                    There are not too many people around,
                        walking
                                ,with their opinions on hand
                                                    : "Art!
                                    for Art's sake!"


(And i think;
            How difFerent this is
                        from, "SomeWhere Else"
        where, a Soldier would demand
                        for the same kind of rights
                                    In a foreign land,
                                    dressed in camouflaged fatigues
                                    with an Uzi
                                        slung over his shoulder,
                                                        say
                                                        ing
                        "YOUR PAPERS!  YOUR
                        PAPERS!  LET ME SEE YOUR PAPERS!!!")
, except
for those    , mostly
in cars
going home
from the long days
they've just lived
in the lengths
of their lives
            /tired
from the things
that they do

with their lives,
And/ThereForeTheyAreInGreatHurRies(

                              Be . . . .lieveIt!
                              Be . . . .lieveIt!
                                 YouBetteRBe . . . .lieveIt!
                                       Be . . . .lieveIt!)

Nonchalantly tossing
lighted cigarettes
from out their
open windows
                 watching
the world go
down the drain(
                 bye)
stepping harder
on the gas
when they see
the lights
turning
from yellow, to red,
                 They
already traveling
beyond the speed
of anybody walking,
trying desperately
to be
the first to
get
to
the other side
of a brand new street

which they've seen
before,
at the corner
of which
are
2POLICE
& 1 blacKDude
imprisoned in a trance
& a light
turning
from yellow, to ReD!
                    (My little sister says
                              about her visit with me here:
                                        "The lights don't give you enough ti)me
                                        to
                                        chew yo
                                        ur gum
                                        &cross the
                                        street!"
                                             , She
                    coming from a real Cool/CRUeL Metropolis
                    having thus acquired an acute UNderstanding
                    of the danger of crossing a simple street,
                                             for a girl, She says
                         *"As soon as you step out to cross it,*
                         *The lights start blinking for you to go back!*
                         *It's a car's world out here!*
                         *Pedestrians should drive!"*
                                        TheBlack peDestrianMan
                                                  sits

In the POLICEMAN's CAR
with his BiGBlacKHanDs
                              down
in front of HiM
                    moping,
                sort of
For TheCAUSE! of his BlacKsKiN
                                        —THaT

though it blended with
the color of this NiGHT,
                              It failed
to cloak HiM from THEIR SiGHT!


And
THEPOLICE,
WoMan,
LaDy,
CoP,
is sitting in the front seat
                    (preTending)
                        that it is Her duTy
                            to be DOing her nails
                                        ,While
                    holding on to the leather of herGun,
                                        touchingIt,
                                    ListeninG . . . . . . . . . . . . . . . . . . . . . . . . . . . . . . . . . . . .
        To Every ThoughT that HE has
        To Think
                    :This BlackMan,
                        HiS Black Pride, Fuming
                                        within

hiS BlackMan's Feelings

               (sitting
               in the back
               seat
               of a
               STraNGeMaN's
               CaR!)

Outside,
   The Air is Cool . . . .
          :Thus is San Diego,
               A City most noticeable for
                  Its Lovely Days
                    of
                  Perfect Skies
                     (iF
  you ignore the factories
        where BomBs are born
 & Therefore, THE TARGET
       That carpets the floOR)
           , And ToNighT . . .
                is a beautiful night
                   To Be Lived
             & enjoy in your being!

THEMANCoP
     rests languidly,
       leaning against the
       roof of his car
         ,Observing the tranquility
          of a RedLightDIstriCT's ACtiVity

                                    ReMarKing,
                    "How smoothly America funCtions
                                    free from Crime,
                                                    at
                                    Peace" (
                    while, POLItICIans seek Votes
                            in the childish arms
                    of
                            loving prostitutes)


THEMANCoP calls
            THEBoYS
                , Back at the Ranch
                    To see how the BallGame is going
                                        — & if anybody thoughT
                                            to leave him a sandwich
                                            for when things go BORinG
                    , And while he's at it
                                (& picking his teeth with a knife)
                    He asks THIS COMPUTER
                                    THEY'VE got over there (with a VoICE like a woMan
                                                of aNAnDRoGyNous souND)
                    If sHE'S
                        Ever Heard of this WiseGuy
                                        HE'S got
                                            in the backseat of the Car/
                            If "HE" EverEver
                                        ,Ever Did
                            AnyThing!
                            AnyThing, WronG
                    In HiS Whole Loving Life/

AnyThing/AnyThing!
As aBlackMan/Child
in this World
WITHaCRIMINALMIND!
—Anything, Anything!
*"Are You Sure?!*
*—What's The Score?!"*

THE ANSWER IS:... NO!!!.../&/SO!!!...

THEMANCoP must write HiM a ticket, According to
"TheProPerProCeDurE"
(Thinking)
:If this were a windy city
HE'D run HiM in
for spittininthegutter!
...&TOHELL!
WITHtHEWoMEN
SCReeeEEEEaMINGGGINALLEYS(
some)
Reluctantly,losing,virginities
,while
the blood of their taxes
pays
the way
forthewagesofSin
&Preachers
are left
arguING
withtheMeanFaceoftheWind!

Now, THEMANCoP calls
            TheBlacK, bOY
to come out
from out
of the car,
            realeasy, like slow
And sign Here
On the line
To say
That I
Gave yoU
This,
And ThaT
YoU
Took IT
And, Now
U
N
D
E
R
S
T
A
N
D
ThaT
YoU Owe
"The
Good
PeoPle"

Of
This
Fare
City,
      Truly
      America's Finest
      Fair City,
35 Bucks
Of
Your
Hard Earned
How
Ever
It
Is
That
YoU
Get
IT
Cold
Cash,
BECAUSE!!!!!!!!!!!!!!!!!!!!!!!!!!!!!!!!!!!!!!!!!!!!!!!!!!!!!!!!!!!!!!!!!!!!!!!!!!!!!!!!!!!!!!!!!!!!!!!!!!!!!!!!!!!!!!!!!!!!!!!!!!!!!!!!!!!!!!!!!!!!!!!!!
YoU *DiD*
Cross
The
Street
While
The YelloW
LighT
Was
A-BlinK-InG

And, Then
*DiD*
Turn
A-ReD
By
The Time
YoU-A-GoT
To
The
Other
Good Side!
And, So HE Signs
HiS NaMe!..
On
The
Paper:
The NaMe…
HiS Mother
Gave
To HiM,
The NaMe!…
By Which
He Is
KnowN
On
The
Face
Of
This Earth,
The NaMe!…
By

Which
GOD
Will Know
HiM
As Well:
CAPITAL X!
And HiS Fingers
are All on the pen!
      O!HiSBlacKFinGerS'PrinTS!
Are On
The Piece of Paper
And On
The Hood of The Car
And On
The Back of The Seat
Where HE WePT
HiS TeaRS
And
HiS TeaRS
Are NoW LeFT
Where
HiS ShAdOW
Once Sulked
And, For This
Even IT!
Refuses
to
walk
with
him
just now, No

not now
It fades
in
the
depth
of
This Night,
      *"OH! WHERE IS HOME?!"*

             …THEMANCoP
               gives HiM
               TheTickeT
               withPride,
               like a piece of ArT
               but it aint,
               TearingiT
                from out of a book
                of them.


And, NoW, "THE COMPUTER"
Has Devoured HiS NaMe!…
           And, *"SomeWhere,"* *"SomeWhere!"*
          No One Knows Where
                   — It is smacking its lips
                     & waiting for dessert!


AND IT WILL NEVER FORGET!

NO! IT WILL NEVER FORGET:
The NaMe!…Nor/the/Height/of/Said/MaN
Nor the Weight of HiM
Nor the Color of HiS Eyes

Nor the Color of HiS Hair
Nor the Color of HiS Skin
Nor the Number that isHis
Nor The Age of This MaN as He Ages
Through Time
                —This BlacKMaN
                            ¿WHO?
                                    …at 2:30 in the morning/ One
                                                dark and lonely, Good Morning!
        was detained by THEPOLICE
                            BECAUSE!!!!!!!!!!!!!!!!!!!!!!!!!!!!!!!!!!!!!!!!!!!!!!!!!!!!!!!!!!!!!!!!!!!!!!!!!!!!!!!!!!!!!!!!!!!!!!!!!!
!!!!!!!!!!!!!!!!!!!!!!!!!!!!!!!!!!!!!!!!!!!!!!!!!!!!!!!!!!!!"The 'DistinCtive' Color
!!!!!!!!!!!!!!!!!!!!!!!!!!!!!!!!!!!!!!!!!!!!!!!!!!!!!!!!!!!!of a LighT
!!!!!!!!!!!!!!!!!!!!!!!!!!!!!!!!!!!!!!!!!!!!!!!!!!!!!!!!!!!!was
!!!!!!!!!!!!!!!!!!!!!!!!!!!!!!!!!!!!!!!!!!!!!!!!!!!!!!!!!!!!AGaINST/HiM!"


We Must Be Thankful ThaT
                ThE DiFfErEncE, HeRe
                            ,from AnyWhere ElSe
                                        In This World (is)
    ThaTThisBlacKMaNis
                , Finally set,
                        on the leash of his  f ,  reedom to go
                        about,D,oing his   bu, si, ness        in
                        pursui,    t     of               the
                        ha,pp,y,n,es,s he  dreams, in his  w i
                        d   e,      o    p    e      n,m i  n  d
                                                — AnyWhere ,ElSe
HE WOULD HAVE BEEN SHOT • RIGHT ON THE SPOT • FOR BREAKING THE LAW!!!

So, TheNicePOLICEMANWoMANCoPs

having, Thus
        Completed Their DuTy,
                drive away, with their lights
                              swallowed up
                  in the eyes of the monster
                          ,Whom(?)
            They've Sworn:
                ToProTecT&ToSerVe
                WithTheirLives. . .   Owns
                        the
                  world
              going
            round

&TheBlacKMaN,     goes
            slowly, across the street
                  (contemplating ,This)


                ANDTHELIGHTSHAVENOMOREOPINIONTOUTTERINHISFACE!
BuT NoW!!!——— HE IS CURRRRRRRRRRRRRRRRRRRRRRSSSSSiNG!!!. . .
POuNDING theAiROfTHiSNIGhT——————————————————— with HiS VoICE!:
I-KNOW-I'M-NOT-WHITE!!!-I-KNOW-I'M-NOT-WHITE!!!-I-KNOW-I'M-NOT-WHITE!!!-I-KNOW-I'M-NOT-
WHITE!!!-I-KNOW-I'M-NOT-WHITE!!!-I-KNOW-I'M-NOT-WHITE!!!-I-KNOW-I'M-NOT-WHITE!!!-I-KNOW-I'M-
NOT-WHITE!!!-I-KNOW-I'M-NOT-WHITE!!!-I-KNOW-I'M-NOT-WHITE!!!-I-KNOW-I'M-NOT-WHITE!!!-I-KNOW-
I'M-NOT-WHITE!!!-I-KNOW-I'M-NOT-WHITE!!!-I-KNOW-I'M-NOT-WHITE!!!-I-KNOW-I'M-NOT-WHITE!!!-I-
KNOW-I'M-NOT-WHITE!!!-I-KNOW-I'M-NOT-WHITE!!!-I-KNOW-I'M-NOT-WHITE!!!-I-KNOW-I'M-NOT-WHI-
TE!!!-I-KNOW-I'M-NOT-WHITE!!!-I-KNOW-I'M-NOT-WHITE!!!-I-KNOW-I'M-NOT-WHITE!!!-I-KNOW-I'M-NOT-
WHITE!!!-I-KNOW-I'M-NOT-WHITE!!!-I-KNOW-I'M-NOT-WHITE!!!-I-KNOW-I'M-NOT-WHITE!!!-I-KNOW-I'M-
NOT-WHITE!!!-I-KNOW-I'M-NOT-WHITE!!!-I-KNOW-I'M-NOT-WHITE!!!-I-KNOW-I'M-NOT-WHITE!!!-I-KNOW-
I'M-NOT-WHITE!!!-I-KNOW-I'M-NOT-WHITE!!!-I-KNOW-I'M-NOT-WHITE!!!-I-KNOW-I'M-NOT-WHITE!!!-
I-KNOW-I'M-NOT-WHITE!!!-I-KNOW-I'M-NOT-WHITE!!!-I-KNOW-I'M-NOT-WHITE!!!-I-KNOW-I'M-NOT-
WHITE!!!-I-KNOW-I'M-NOT-WHITE!!!-I-KNOW-I'M-NOT-WHITE!!!-I-KNOW-I'M-NOT-WHITE!!!-I-KNOW-I'M-

NOT-WHITE!!!-I-KNOW-I'M-NOT-WHITE!!!-I-KNOW-I'M-NOT-WHITE!!!-I-KNOW-I'M-NOT-WHITE!!!-I-KNOW-I'M-NOT-WHITE!!!-I-KNOW-I'M-NOT-WHITE!!!-I-KNOW-I'M-NOT-WHITE!!!-I-KNOW-I'M-NOT-WHITE!!!-I-KNOW-I'M-NOT-WHITE!!!-I-KNOW-I'M-NOT-WHITE!!!-I-KNOW-I'M-NOT-WHITE!!!-I-KNOW-I'M-NOT-WHITE!!!-I-KNOW-I'M-NOT-WHITE!!!-I-KNOW-I'M-NOT-WHITE!!!-I-KNOW-I'M-NOT-WHITE!!!-I-KNOW-I'M-NOT-WHITE!!!-I-KNOW-I'M-NOT-WHITE!!!-I-KNOW-I'M-NOT-WHITE!!!-I-KNOW-I'M-NOT-WHITE!!!-I-KNOW-I'M-NOT-WHITE!!!-I-KNOW-I'M-NOT-WHITE!!!-I-KNOW-I'M-NOT-WHITE!!!-I-KNOW-I'M-NOT-WHITE!!!-I-KNOW-I'M-NOT-WHITE!!!-I-KNOW-I'M-NOT-WHITE!!!-I-KNOW-I'M-NOT-WHITE!!!-I-KNOW-I'M-NOT-WHITE!!!-I-KNOW-I'M-NOT-WHITE!!!-I-KNOW-I'M-NOT-WHITE!!!-I-KNOW-I'M-NOT-WHITE!!!-I-KNOW-I'M-NOT-WHITE!!!--I-KNOW-I'M-NOT-WHITE!!!-I-KNOW-I'M-NOT-WHITE!!!-I-KNOW-I'M-NOT-WHITE!!!-I-KNOW-I'M-NOT-WHITE!!!-I-KNOW-I'M-NOT-WHITE!!!-I-KNOW-I'M-NOT-WHITE!!!-I-KNOW-I'M-NOT-WHITE!!!-I-KNOW-I'M-NOT-WHITE!!!-I-KNOW-I'M-NOT-WHITE!!!-I-KNOW-I'M-NOT-WHITE!!!-I-KNOW-I'M-NOT-WHITE!!!-I-KNOW-I'M-NOT-WHITE!!!-I-KNOW-I'M-NOT-WHITE!!!-I-KNOW-I'M-NOT-WHITE!!!-I-KNOW-I'M-NOT-WHITE!!!-I-KNOW-I'M-NOT-WHITE!!!-I-KNOW-I'M-NOT-WHITE!!!-I-KNOW-I'M-NOT-WHITE!!!-I-KNOW-I'M-NOT-WHITE!!!-I-KNOW-I'M-NOT-WHITE!!!-I-KNOW-I'M-NOT-WHITE!!!-I-KNOW-I'M-NOT-WHITE!!!--I-KNOW-I'M-NOT-WHITE!!!-I-KNOW-I'M-NOT-WHITE!!!-I-KNOW-I'M-NOT-WHITE!!!-I-KNOW-I'M-NOT-WHITE!!!-I-KNOW-I'M-NOT-WHITE!!!-I-KNOW-I'M-NOT-WHITE!!!-I-KNOW-I'M-NOT-WHITE!!!-I-KNOW-I'M-NOT-WHITE!!!-I-KNOW-I'M-NOT-WHITE!!!-I-KNOW-I'M-NOT-WHITE!!!-I-KNOW-I'M-NOT-WHITE!!!I-KNOW-I'M-NOT-WHITE!!!-I-KNOW-I'M-NOT-WHITE!!!-I-KNOW-I'M-NOT-WHITE!!!I-KNOW-I'M-NOT-WHITE!!!-I-KNOW-I'M-NOT-WHITE!!!-I-KNOW-I'M-NOT-WHITE!!!I-KNOW-I'M-NOT-WHITE!!!-I-KNOW-I'M-NOT-WHITE!!!-I-KNOW-I'M-NOT-WHITE!!!I-KNOW-I'M-NOT-WHITE!!!-I-KNOW-I'M-NOT-WHITE!!!-I-KNOW-I'M-NOT-WHITE!!!

# ELOQUENT HYPOCRISY

We come to the Courtroom,
           the room
              where Court is to be heard—
              where Justice
                    supposedly, will get a word

To see Ourselves
         enSlaved again,
    answering to a System
    that professes Justice,
           while knowingly
              owing Us
        much more
        than it is willing
           to pay:
              the cost of
                lost human lives;
        unwilling to admit
              to its own kind of crimes…

And Here we are:
      the beautifully arrayed
       Latino-Africano faces
      of beaten, torn
          men & women(
            some with
              their children)
      Torn, from our native lands
                 , distant

                                          as memory
                    Forced, by the slick trickery
                                    of democracy
                    to bow & cower
                       to a bunch of lies,
                                          told
                    by a bunch of liars—
                                    Be they *Black* or
                                                *White,*
                              who told them!!!

Oh, Yes!
   They *do* have *Us* on their sides
                                    , confused
         into believing
                  that because they let us now
                  wear their uniforms
                                    , dressed
              in the plain clothes
                           of *Them*
         We are *one* of *Them,* are
              with *Them;*
                       Loved
                  by *Them*—
                           A-*Credit*
                  to our Race
                                , in Complicity
                  with the Crimes
                           of their hate...

Look across the rows
    of the calmly seated,
        falsely accused gathered here,
                Today
  And you *jusT*
    see *Us;*
        Once proud warriors
      sitting with our arms
       folded across
         our Eurocentrically dressed
             Chests!
                Gone, are the handmade
                     trinkets
              that protected Us once;
            Gone, are the beliefs
             that held us in a united
                 song
                  of a Spiritual Truth.

Instead, now
    our minds' eyes
  are focused on
      the *Idolized Ideals*
    of other men,
  Who used them
      to capture
       & shackle Us, even
        unto this postmodern day—
             as it dawns upon
              the beginning of a new
        millennium year

of Man's Life on
Earth!
Ruling over
"the dominion which GOD
himSelf
has given him"
, so say *They*
who oppress
as they pray
, while their morals
colLide
with thefaceof *theTruth.*

And, *Why are we here?*
(We ask of ourselves)
, aLoud
while in the privacy
of our minds
... we think;
The subtle reason, as
bright as a new falling star
: *Because of who we are!*
We failed
, they say
to pay
our way
into the subterranean death of *Their* way
— a theft
of a measly
2bucks&75cents
— SmallChange

conSidered
anyWhere in this world
toDay...

But Where,
O Where, is the compensation
for the cost of
Their Crimes
— Committed
throughout ancient
& now modern times?
— Nowhere
to be seen
are tears
for their suffering peers—
Just, the panic of
the rest of the world
living in fear
of eXtinction!

Make clear the distinCtion!—
Who lights the candle
to light up the way?!...
Who Is It Among Us
Who burns Frankincense & Myrrh
for the Memory of
our Elders & Ancestors;
For those
who suffered before Us,
For being just like Us

                                                    : *Black,* as the Day
                                                          beGrudgingly
                                                    gives way to the Night.

Woe!
     Surely, Not Those among Us
                              *Who*
               have given up
                              *our Cause*
          to wear *Their* shields
                              , without honor
          & take pride in
            *Their* red badges
                    of cowardly courage—
Not *They;*
          The lost warriors
                    of our tribes
          *Who* are now
          forever on *Their* sides/
                         Against *Us,*
               Who arrest *Us;*
                              Who
                    bring *Us*
                         In,
                    handCuffed,
                              bearing
                    FalseWitness
               to the Justice
                    *They* Serve!…
                                        NO!
                                   Not *They!*

*They, Who*
     have lost
  the Know-how
          to *Bow*
            to *Our Kind of GODS!*

# JADED ON JADE

Since the youth has grown
  from infancy
    & it has learned
     that all the streets, are not
      lined in gold;
           Thus
             they create their own
      kind of *shimmer*
          by breaking bottles
           & any other types of glass,
                      todust...

So that as we view
    the naked streets,
             They glisten as we speak
  & walk
    through the valleys of crime;
                Yea, our eyes
                    as closed as being blind, yet
     Not victimless
         : Teenagers
           drinking the malt liquors, which their
           politically incorrect idols advertise
           for sponsors of their genres who live
           well elsewhere, where they hide,
           as uncontrollably intoxicated youth
           hallucinate they're drinking champagne
           bubbles underage—

                              And just as soon as
                    they're through with their hefty 40-Oz
                    bottles of brew, they quickly smash them
                    to the ground— wherever they are
                    standing there, as if tossing
                    fine crystal glasses in the air
                    violently into a fireplace
                    where burns a rage out of control
                    inextinguishable in their imagination!!!

              In fact,
                    Infested too
                          with the shrill illness
                                of unconcern
                                      that does not itself discern
                          *Ignorance*
                                from lessons learned.

So how far have we really come?!
                    ThaT
        Our children still solve their problems
                                with a gun (
              and shun the brightness
                          *, revealing*
              the ever present likeness
                          Shining down on everyone,
                    yet still distinguishing each
                    from each, & one from one
                                )uniquely each
                                      just as unique…


100    JESÚS PAPOLETO MELÉNDEZ

*Thus...*
This is the role *the Youth,*
our children, play—
That which we show them
& model each day...
*O, You can Blame Them*—
If you must,
But, in fact, it's from Us
, with our *un*caring
in*Difference*
to individual's strife,
That *They* learn how it is
to live Life.

# KILLKILLKILL

*KILLKIILLKIIILLL!!!...*

The KuKluxKlan wears a badge on its Chest —
SaiD!
The KuKluxKlan wears a badge on its Breasts
And Thus, it profess
To Stand for Justice
In The U.S. of A —
*HeyHey!*
*HeyHeyHey!*
— SaiD! ...


The KuKluxKlan's taken over the Land
dressed as the PoliceMan
to Kill
The BlackNiggerMan&
The Spic/Puerto Rican
And ALL
that it can
kill
He will
kill...
killKill
killKill   Kill
killKill
*Hey!*
*YeahYeah!...*

I Say...

The Police just shot another kid this week
Statistics reaching new high peaks
Just shot another kid this week, in
The back of his stomach?!

Said,
he was running away, toward them
wielding a knife, or a snake —
And if it was a snake, it was one of *Those*
that spewed fire from its nostrils
& had teeth instead of fangs,
as sharp as Sharks'
And he looked scary in the dark
So they shot — They shot
They shot him dead!

And I Said!...

The KuKluxKlan wears a badge on its Chest
                      & a BuLLet-Proof Vest
                          That shows no respect
                              for none of the oppressed
                                     , while
                  No One Protests
                   'Cause they live with Regret
                    for the Checks that they get
                — To Play DeaD!!!

*YeahYeah!…*
*YeahYeah!…*
*YeahYeahYeah!…*
i SaiD!…

Suddenly the 12-year-old
Is TwelveFEEtTALL
And has an Arm that propels
a barrage of Machete Missiles at free will
whose blades come out spinning
in great spirals of death!

So they shot him through
the back
of his chest —
Shattering his neck!

Though no weapon
was ever found
He died
faced down
in his blood on the ground…

Dead to the bone!
*Another*NiGGer*ALONE!!!*

'Cause The KKK loves to KillKill&Kill
freely at will
& surely They will
while our peoPle
sit still
in the cells

of themselves
*en*slaved in their selves,
Killing
themSelves
In the projects
Where they dwell —
*in* their own kind of hell!
*YeahYeah!...*
*Yeah   Yeah!...*
*Oh,YeahYeahYeah!...*
I SaiD!...

*'Cause 'Cuz, 'Cause Bloods(*
*sheD) —*

The KuKluxKlan is now the *Voice of the Land*
That speaks firmly
with a violent Right Hand!
*'Lest you forget —*
*It kills, lacking respect*
*For the low-life human insects*
*Of the cultural sect*
*Our skin color represents*
*Which they hate & resent;*
*Thus, they see Us far less*
*Useless*
*than domesticated pets;*
*Mere subhuman insects*
*Which they must dissect*
*, like any other pests*

They detest
                — Oh Yes!
                        YesYes!
                        YesYes!


...For The KuKluxKlan,
                dressed-up like the local Police,
                are armed to the teeth,
& marching in time
    With the Element of Crime
                        Cause they represent
                        All the EXTrEmEELEmEnts
                        Of a FacistGovernment
                        Where your vOtes count
                                — But don't represent!...


Believe what my friends
                say in the West Coast
For They know
                Who hates them
                        The Most:
    "If you got a problem
                        & you call THE POLICE,
        Then you got 2 problems
                        to deal with at least!"


'Cause The KuKluxKlan's taken over the Land
                        dressed as the PoliceMan
                                to Kill

The BlackNiggerMan&
The Spic/Puerto Rican
And ALL
that it can
kill…
He will
kill
killKill
killKill  Kill  killKill !!!…
KillerKopsKillkill  &Kill
killKill !!!…
&Shots!…
ShotsShots, &Shots!  ShootShots, KillerKops
Shot  ShotKopShootsKops  KopsShotsShootShots
ShotsShotKillKopsShotShootKops!
&WhatNot/*Shots*Stop!
…*'Though*
The KuKluxKlan wears a badge on its Breasts
And Thus, it profess
To Stand for Justice
In The U.S. of A —
*HeyHey!!*
*HeyHeyHey!!!*
Said!

# THE FLOOD CAME TO PUERTO RICO

The flood came to Puerto Rico/
unexpected/    unwelcome
like american tourists
& it left    like american tourists:
taking all & leaving nothing.

the flood came to Puerto Rico/
& with it came geologists
        /they are trying to find new names
        for the many lakes & rivers
        that now exist
        where towns once were
        where homes once stood
        where people once lived
        where children once played
        in the warmth of afternoon suns
        where the beautiful culture
        that is mine once sang    sang
        its loveliness over the hills & mountains.

the flood came to Puerto Rico/
& american airlines are taking pictures
for their advertisements of their new lagoons
where the kennedy family will vacation
this summer/    next summer
all year round.

the flood came to Puerto Rico/
killing my people
drowning them in a new form
of oppression/
leaving them jobless/    homeless
to the mercy of american kindness
with begging hands in the air
with tears in their eyes
with crying & dying babies
in their arms/
    leaving them with less
    than what they were known
     to ever have

        lost/
          separated from
            their mutual loves.


the flood came to Puerto Rico/
& with it came the red cross
             /after the flood
to search for *Donald Trump's** golf courses
          & summer homes.


*{The original 1971 version reads: "rockefeller's summer home."}

# TO PAY A NATIONAL DEBT — TO PUERTO RICO OSCAR LÓPEZ-RIVERA MUST BE SET FREE IMMEDIATELY!

*Para Mí Pueblo Puertorriqueño*

TO BEGIN to eradicate the massive money debt
  That's larger than the population of Coquís globally
      — that's owed Puerto Rico
          by the United States
               *in the Americas*—
Our Brother Nuestro,
        *Oscar López-Rivera*
    *debería Be Set Free Immediately*
      from the penitentiary that incarcerates Him
                , like Jesús Cristo
                    — *Illegally!!!*

For it is *THEY*—
    The United States *in the Americas*
          — & NOT *HE,*
            *Oscar López-Rivera*
Who are guilty of the most heinous Crimes Against Humanity
as is proved by the slavery of Puerto Rico,
the last recognized colony in modern history:
The acculturation of our Island Nation
into an assimilation of Cultural Self-Hatred—
A family fractured into disunity,
Displaced from Native lands into Public Housing Projects;
From Bosques to Barrios, Finqueros to Homelessness
While each day we bury more elders, turned ancestors
Transitioning to Saints of our Diaspora.

*The Gentrifying Dawn Rises over El Barrio mío...*
foreboding in shadows stretching from East Harlem, south to
Loisaida; to La Perla; to la Boca de Cangrejos en Ponce...
As the young Entrepreneurial Millennial conga-despising Interlopers
emerge in El Barrio from subway tunnels at 110th Street
*y* Lexingtón Avenue, Looking for *"SpaHa!"*
Now walking around the community dragging
airport luggage carriers, seeking to decipher the address scribbled
on a piece of paper; The new-sublet apartments,
"AirBnB in El Barrio," while disappearing Botánicas(
like missing teeth from a mouth dying of decay)
& Bodegas going out of business, turned Ultrasuper-Supermarkets,
still selling *Coladores* for Bustelo Café, & Universal Product-
Coded *Votive Candles;* while *Santeros* bagging groceries
for chump change, go looking for Temp-work outside
their fields of expertisé!

THE PROFIT CULTURE-VULTURE VENTURE CAPITALISTS,
THE CARPET BAGGERS OF ROBBER-BARON HEDGE FUND TRUSTS
Who P.R.O.M.E.S.A.'d to be trusted, and came instead
To steal in the bright, Caribbean Daylight,
And steal away in the dark, Capitalistic broad Night—
Feeling the Right for the Might of the United States
*in the Americas* Banking Laws—
replete with legal flaws designed to defraud the poor;
Evincing a design to colonize through humiliation,
Allowing for the experimentation of forced sterilization
upon our Puerto Rican women without their knowledge(
much less their consent) while their brothers, cousins
and husbands were sent off to go fight & die

in the rice fields of Viet Nam,
Where Brother *Oscar López-Rivera* had to survive—
                                                    And did!
And came home having been awarded the Bronze Star for Bravery
in a war that opened up his eyes to what Americans Fight For
In the name of the Freedom they so freely adore,
While their Allies & Navies cowardly dropped Bombs
upon our baby islands Vieques y Culebras—
                                                    ¡Y Que!
Where now radioactive beachfront condominiums & bungalows
are being sold to the sons of bitches & daughters of the newly riché,
Who *Bill* the exploited on *Our Madre Isla* for the cost incurred
for the exploitation of the Nation we no longer own!

Hypocrisy, being the Mother & Father of all Sin,
Is opposed by Righteousness, its opposite, in its own righteous skin—
That despises Injustice, Prejudice & Racism
for preventing the Human Spirit to sing!!!!…
My Boricua Soul cries out in anguish!—
Diametrically opposed in English & in Spanish
to being juxtaposed between a cultural complexity
in this concrete city and a tropical repose that contradicts
the imposition of an imposturous Democracy—
Killing our People through a program of atrocious attrition
While you, *Oscar López-Rivera,* a Patriot, are imprisoned for Sedition—
Paying the price of Freedom, as it so very often demands
the loss of one's Liberty!

Oh, Yes!
     I've seen the best minds of Our Generations'
                                                    — Incarceration!

For committing a crime in a criminal society that steals
the best of our progeny for petty larceny, turned into
Indentured Servitude for the Corporate State Full of Hate.

That's why *Oscar López-Rivera* Must Be Set Free—
Because you're the example of the Puerto Rican Brother-Man, Sir
that we need walking around replenishing our community.
You are an authentic brother— as true as a Poet,
Uncompromisingly dedicated to The Truth being told.
We hold you up as our Self-Esteem, a pillar of the Integrity
of the Soul's Sovereignty—
In your Strength, we finally find *this* Unity
Because you've made a sacrifice of the Most Supreme—
To give your Life-blood in pursuit of *The Puerto Rican Dream— Liberty!*
Which is why You Must Be Freed!

What we need now is un Nuevo Movimiento Patrimonio
Para to save the histórico-artístico cultura de Puerto Rico
made by our artists con amor, por valor y sacrificio:
A Vanguard of Artists— Armed to the teeth!
Who've beaten their *pens & paintbrushes* into
WEAPONS OF MASS DESTRUCTION
To retrieve our National & Natural Treasures
Before the *"Artifacts for Sale"* Fire-Sale of the history
of Puerto Rico and its People en el Caribe,
Puts an end to the proud legacy of Los Tainos
Once and for all!

¡Ay! Mí Pueblo Puertorriqueño!
¡Ay! Mí Diaspora Nuyoricana!

¿AREN'T— THEY— WORTH— FIGHTING— FOR?

¿WHAT— ARE— WE— WAITING— FOR?
¡FOR-THEM TO TAKE AWAY OUR PLAYAS Y PAIS!
¿FOR-WHAT?

> *To payback for being a Colony for 118 years!*
>
> *¡Pal Carajó!...*

For, as Don Pedro Albizu Campos would like to say—
  *"¡To cualquir Fulano, o Fulana de Tal—o Charlatán!..."*
WE REJECT YOUR CHAPTER 9,
    and, *influenced by Afro-Cuban Jazz,*
      WE GO STRAIGHT-AHEAD TO CHAPTER 10:
This is the Goddamned End!
It's either— *Revolution* or Civil War!
Whichever one intends to restore our Dignity and Sovereignty!
To once again prove to the Imperialists of the World, that—
Although we are an island-nation,
                    We are nevertheless A Nation
  of a proudly fierce and courageous people
Who will chuck a poisoned-spear right through your evil, greedy,
Conquistadores hearts!

For, If told be The Truth: *In War—*
It's always "an Eye for an Eye, & a Tooth for a Tooth"
Regardless of *Who* has *The Truth* on its side!
Believe it or not—Wars are fought in parking lots & bus stops
& shopping malls & baseball parks;
Terrorism *is* Economic-Sanctions imposed by the powerless, &
Freedom Fighters are as *"Terroristic"* as Founding Fathers!!!
For the mythology of *AmeriKKKa's* history is as bloody as
                    *The Passion of Christ!*
                    — For Christ's Sake!

And, *That* is why
> We must Free *Oscar López-Rivera* Now!
*We Must Free this Brother!...*
> Because!!!
>> as Life-blood running through our veins
> *"Our Mother is the Same;*
>> *Her Name is Borinkén!"*

# A CONVERSATION WITH MY SON

*(for Wazuri-Gente Meléndez)*

Let us draw a Map of the World
It would be a Pyramid with many levels of
people, each holding another level of peo
ple above their level, on the bottom
would be the poor, that's to be ex
pected, below them would be no
thing, above them would be a
smaller group of people, hol
ding up yet another small
er group of people, hold
ing up yet another
smaller group of
people, holding
up yet anoth
er smaller
group of
people
Above
the
poor
would
be  the
middle
poor, below
the upper poor,
below the richer

poor, who are above
the police, who are below
the lower rich, below the mi
ddle rich, below the upper rich,
below the rich, below the Govern
ment & Religion, below the Truly Rich
Below
GOD

# FAIR FOR FARE

Today I saw
    a poet
   panhandling poems
 in a subway train,
         subterranean
         beneath
           a bustling city
            of flashing lights

Sandwich-boarded
        between
 a poem
   & advertisement
         , decrying
        homelessness

Reading from
   the scribbling prose
        upon a page
   in a composition
       notebook,

Apologizing
    that celebrity & fame
    are not equated
       quite the same
    as is fortune & fame;
Thus, promising
    to *"pay it forward"*
  whenever life on Earth
       improves,

He croons
in perfect Iambic pentameter
against
The roaring railing
wheels
against the steel
of Reality
& Life—
Against a will
Against the wind,
Against the word
Against the world.

# OVERFLOW

*Someone* said:
            *The Streets of the Promised*
                                    *Land*
                *are Lined in Gold.*

Oh, I have lived there,
                Yeah...
    Their streets over*flow*
                    in gold
      :That's so much blood
        our youth
            has *spilt*.

# ACKNOWLEDGEMENTS

❖ ❖ ❖

"A Conversation with a Blind Man"
*Concertos on Market Street* (Kenetic Images, 1993)

"A Conversation With My Son"
*A Gathering of the Tribes Literary Journal* (No. 17, 1979)

"A San Diego Southern/African Night"
Manteca, An Anthology of Afro-LAtin@ Poets (Arte Publico Press, 2017)
In Defense of Mumia (Writers and Readers Publishing, 1996)
*Concertos on Market Street* (Kenetic Images, 1993)

"eLoquent Hypocrisy"
*Poets America* (Hidden Clearing Books, 2014)
*phati'tude Literary Magazine* (1998)

"The Flood Came to Puerto Rico"
*Pa'lante a La luz—Charge into The Light* (Rogue Scholars Press, 2018)
*Hey Yo! Yo Soy! 40 Years of Nuyorican Street Poetry* (2Leaf Press, 2012)
*Centro, Journal for Puerto Rican Studies (Centro de Estudios Puertorriqueños)*, Hunter College, City University of New York (Spring 1988)
*Have you Seen Liberation* (Fieldston School of Ethical Culture, 1972)

"Human Wisdom"
*Not Black and White—Inside Words* (Bronx WritersCorps, 1996)

"Story From A Mountain"
*Centro, Journal for Puerto Rican Studies (Centro de Estudios Puertorriqueños),* Hunter College,
    City University of New York (Spring 1988)
*Peace is Our Profession* (East River Press, 1981)
*Maiz* (San Diego State University, 1981)
*Herejes Y Mitificadores* (Ediciones Huracan, 1980)

"Tourism Up/Dow Jones 6 pts."
*Long Shot Literary Journal* (Vol. 18, Long Shot Publications, 1996)
*Not Black and White—Inside* (Bronx WritersCorps, 1996)
*Centro, Journal for Puerto Rican Studies (Centro de Estudios Puertorriqueños),* Hunter College,
    City University of New York (Spring 1988)
*La Linea Quebrada / The Broken Line* (Border Arts Publication, 1987)

"Unity Speak"
*Poets America* (Hidden Clearing Books, 2014)

# ABOUT THE POET

PHOTO: Carlos David

**JESÚS PAPOLETO MELÉNDEZ** is an award-winning New York-born Puerto Rican poet who is recognized as one of the founders of the Nuyorican Movement. He is also a playwright, teacher and activist.

Affectionately known as "Papo," Meléndez published his first poem, "Message to Urban Sightseers" in *Talkin' About Us* (1969). The publication of his earliest volumes of poetry, *Casting Long Shadows* (1970), *Have You Seen Liberation* (1971), and *Street Poetry & Other Poems* (1972), firmly established Meléndez as a prominent poet in the Nuyorican community. His other publications include *Concertos On Market Street* (Kemetic Images, 1994), which merged his Nuyorican melodies with a Southern California sensibility, and *Hey Yo! Yo Soy! 40 Years of Nuyorican Street Poetry, A Bilingual Edition* (2012) a compilation of his three previously published books from the 1970s. As the recipient of Pregones Theater's 2014 Master Artist

Award, many of the selections from *Hey Yo! Yo Soy!* was made into a play of the same name, and performed at the Puerto Rican Traveling Theater in 2014.

In 1974, Meléndez's play, "The Junkies Stole The Clock," was the first Latino play produced by the New York Shakespeare Festival, The Public Theatre's Nuyorican Playwright's Unit. It was again produced in 1997, and directed by Veronica Caicedo (Caicedo Productions) at the Clemente Soto Vega Cultural Center, in New York City. He also wrote the play, "An Element of Art" (El Porton Theatre Co., 1978).

Beginning in the 1970s, Meléndez began his 40-year career as a poet-facilitator in the public schools, working at workshop programs in California and New York. Meléndez is anthologized most notably in *The Norton Anthology of Latino Literature* (W.W. Norton & Company, 2011); *Bum Rush the Page: A Def Poetry Jam* (Three Rivers Press, 2001); *Literature and Integrated Studies – Forms of Literature* (ScottForesman/HarperCollins Publishers, 1997); *Unsettling America: An Anthology of Contemporary Multicultural Poetry* (Penguin, 1994); *Hojas, Revista de Talleres Literatura* (Universidad Autonoma Baja California, Tijuana, Mexico, 1986); and *Puertoricaner In New York* (Institute for Amerikanerika, Universitat Nurnberg, Germany, 1979). His works were recently published in *Pa'lante a La luz – Charge Into The Light* (Rogue Scholars Press, 2018), *Word, An Anthology by A Gathering of the Tribes* (2017), and *Manteca, An Anthology of Afro-Latin@ Poets* (Arte Publico Press, 2017).

Meléndez is a NYFA Poetry Fellow (New York Foundation for the Arts, 2001), and is the recipient of thr Pregones Theater's 2014 Master Artist Award. He has received the Union Settlement Association "Innovation Award" (2011), the Universes Poetic Ensemble Company Award in "Appreciation of Inspiration & Commitment to the Development of the Company" (2006); The 1st Annual El Reverendo Pedro Pietri Hand Award in Poetry, El Spirit Republic de Puerto Rico, El Puerto Rican Embassy (2006); The Louis Reyes Rivera Lifetime Achievement Award, Amherst College (2004); and an Artist for Community Enrichment (ACE) Award from the Bronx Council on the Arts (1995). Now an elder statesman of the New York poetry scene, Meléndez has become a mentor for emerging poets and writers. ❖

# CONTRIBUTORS

❖ ❖ ❖

PHOTO: Molly Kovel

**JOEL KOVEL**. Professor Emeritus, Bard College, and author of *Enemy of Nature: The End of Capitalism or The End of the World* (2002).

**DEEDEE HALLECK**, Media activist, and author of *Hand Held Visions—The Impossible Possibilities of Community Media* (2001).❖

# OTHER BOOKS BY 2LEAF PRESS

❖ ❖ ❖

2LEAF PRESS challenges the status quo by publishing alternative fiction, non-fiction, poetry and bilingual works by activists, academics, poets and authors dedicated to diversity and social justice with scholarship that is accessible to the general public. 2LEAF PRESS produces high quality and beautifully produced hardcover, paperback and ebook formats through our series: *2LP Explorations in Diversity, 2LP University Books, 2LP Classics, 2LP Translations, Nuyorican World Series,* and *2LP Current Affairs, Culture & Politics.* Below is a selection of 2LEAF PRESS' published titles.

## 2LP EXPLORATIONS IN DIVERSITY

*Substance of Fire: Gender and Race in the College Classroom*
by Claire Millikin
Foreword by R. Joseph Rodríguez, Afterword by Richard Delgado
Contributors Riley Blanks, Blake Calhoun, Rox Trujillo

*Black Lives Have Always Mattered*
*A Collection of Essays, Poems, and Personal Narratives*
Edited by Abiodun Oyewole

*The Beiging of America:*
*Personal Narratives about Being Mixed Race in the 21st Century*
Edited by Cathy J. Schlund-Vials, Sean Frederick Forbes, Tara Betts
with an Afterword by Heidi Durrow

*What Does it Mean to be White in America?*
*Breaking the White Code of Silence, A Collection of Personal Narratives*
Edited by Gabrielle David and Sean Frederick Forbes
Introduction by Debby Irving and Afterword by Tara Betts

## 2LP UNIVERSITY BOOKS

*Designs of Blackness, Mappings in the Literature and Culture of African Americans*
by A. Robert Lee
20TH ANNIVERSARY EXPANDED EDITION

## 2LP CLASSICS

*Adventures in Black and White*
by Philippa Schuyler
Edited and with a critical introduction by Tara Betts

*Monsters: Mary Shelley's Frankenstein and Mathilda*
by Mary Shelley, edited by Claire Millikin Raymond

## 2LP TRANSLATIONS

*Birds on the Kiswar Tree*
by Odi Gonzales, Translated by Lynn Levin
Bilingual: English/Spanish

*Incessant Beauty, A Bilingual Anthology*
by Ana Rossetti, Edited and Translated by Carmela Ferradáns
Bilingual: English/Spanish

## NUYORICAN WORLD SERIES

*Our Nuyorican Thing, The Birth of a Self-Made Identity*
by Samuel Carrion Diaz, with an Introduction by Urayoán Noel
Bilingual: English/Spanish

*Hey Yo! Yo Soy!, 40 Years of Nuyorican Street Poetry,*
*The Collected Works of Jesús Papoleto Meléndez*
Bilingual: English/Spanish

## LITERARY NONFICTION

*No Vacancy; Homeless Women in Paradise*
by Michael Reid

*The Beauty of Being, A Collection of Fables, Short Stories & Essays*
by Abiodun Oyewole

*WHEREABOUTS: Stepping Out of Place,*
*An Outside in Literary & Travel Magazine Anthology*
Edited by Brandi Dawn Henderson

## PLAYS

*Rivers of Women, The Play*
by Shirley Bradley LeFlore, with photographs by Michael J. Bracey

## AUTOBIOGRAPHIES/MEMOIRS/BIOGRAPHIES

*Trailblazers, Black Women Who Helped Make America Great*
*American Firsts/American Icons*
by Gabrielle David
Edited by Carolina Fung Feng

*Mother of Orphans*
*The True and Curious Story of Irish Alice, A Colored Man's Widow*
by Dedria Humphries Barker

*Strength of Soul*
by Naomi Raquel Enright

*Dream of the Water Children:*
*Memory and Mourning in the Black Pacific*
by Fredrick D. Kakinami Cloyd
Foreword by Velina Hasu Houston, Introduction by Gerald Horne
Edited by Karen Chau

*The Fourth Moment: Journeys from the Known to the Unknown, A Memoir*
by Carole J. Garrison, Introduction by Sarah Willis

## POETRY

*PAPOLíTICO, Poems of a Political Persuasion*
by Jesús Papoleto Meléndez
with an Introduction by Joel Kovel and DeeDee Halleck

*Critics of Mystery Marvel, Collected Poems*
by Youssef Alaoui, with an Introduction by Laila Halaby

*shrimp*
by jason vasser-elong, with an Introduction by Michael Castro

*The Revlon Slough, New and Selected Poems*
by Ray DiZazzo, with an Introduction by Claire Millikin

*Written Eye: Visuals/Verse*
by A. Robert Lee

*A Country Without Borders: Poems and Stories of Kashmir*
by Lalita Pandit Hogan, with an Introduction by Frederick Luis Aldama

*Branches of the Tree of Life*
*The Collected Poems of Abiodun Oyewole 1969-2013*
by Abiodun Oyewole, edited by Gabrielle David
with an Introduction by Betty J. Dopson

2Leaf Press is an imprint owned and operated by the Intercultural Alliance of Artists & Scholars, Inc. (IAAS), a NY-based nonprofit organization that publishes and promotes multicultural literature.

NEW YORK
www.2leafpress.org